ALL VALENCIA

Text, photographs, lay-out and reproduction, entirely designed and created by the Technical Department of EDITORIAL ESCUDO DE ORO, S.A.

7th Edition, May 1987

I.S.B.N.

English   84-378-0592-9
German   84-378-0594-5

Dep. Legal B. 16956-1987

editorial **escudo de oro, s.a.** Palaudarias, 26 - 08004 Barcelona - Spain

Impreso en España - Printed in Spain
F.I.S.A. Palaudarias, 26 - 08004 Barcelona

REGIONAL HYMN OF VALENCIA

To pledge Spain new glories,
our Region knew how to fight.
Already in the factories and fields
sound songs of love, hymns of peace!

Make way for the Region
that advances in a triumphal march!

For you the fertile lands
the riches that they store,
and the water murmuring a song of joy
born of the rhythm of Moorish chords.

Art sends her paladins,
offering you their laurels;
and at your feet, Sultaness, my gardens
extend carpets of roses and carnations.

Orange trees of the river banks
burnish their rich treasures;
golden clusters spun beneath
the arches of the palm trees.

The hush of palm trees; the beloved voice
and in a victorious inspired ode;

notes of the aubade
chant the triumph of the Region.

Arise, Valencians!
so that the light
of a new dawn would
greet our voice.

Let our flag brandish
in the air!
Glory to the Fatherland!
Long live Valencia!

Present shield of the city, used since 1377. King Peter the Ceremonious dubbed Valencia a city of dual loyalty, depicted by the two crowned "L's".

VALENTIA · VALENCIA

Valencia, situated in the center of an expansive plain — an irrigated stretch of land — nourished by the river Turia, celebrated in 1962 two thousand years of existence. The historian Tito Livio recounts that the city was founded in the year 138 A.D. by the Roman Consul Junio Bruto and that it had the same name which it bears today: *Valentia*. Some hundred years later, Rome conceded to it the status of colony. An urban center of scant development under the Visigoth monarchy but which in the early times of Muslim domination progressed rapidly until attaining a population of 15,000 inhabitants during the era of Califato of Córdoba; the height of its splendour occurs in the 11th century when it is the seat of the reign of Taifa. The Cid conquered Valencia in 1094 but it again came under Islamic control eight years later, being definitively won over to Christianity in 1238 by the king James I who converted it into the seat of the Valencian Kingdom, one of the states pertaining to the Crown of Aragón. Its progress henceforth was steady and towards 1400 it became the principal city among all of those of the monarchy. Periods of crisis and grandeur followed upon one another with the passing of the years until the present time and until shaping the Valencia that we behold today.

Partial view of Valencia, at dusk. The Gothic Door of Serranos — fortress and arch of triumph — set off by four of the three-hundred belfries that poetically were attributed by Victor Hugo to the city.

THE CATHEDRAL

The Cathedral rises up in the centre of the old part of Valencia. The Episcopal Visigoth Church was located here and later the Moslems built their Mosque on the same site. When the city was taken by James I, work began on the temple, but even with the aid of the citizens it was slow and often interrupted. Initiated under the guise of Gothic Cistercian dictates, work was continued in 1303 incorporating forms of undoubtable French influence. The Sala Capitular was built in the second half of the 14th century (today the Chapel of the Holy Chalice) and the tower of Miguelete was also constructed at that time. The three arches added in 1566 beside the door of the Apostles are done in a Renaissance style, and the Puerta de los Hierros is baroque. The somewhat austere interior of the Cathedral was not to the liking of the people of Valencia of the 18th century, and for that reason it was completely transformed in 1744. The walls were worked on, the arches rounded, the Gothic columns refaced with pilaster, and various relief decorations of a neo-classical style were added. In actual fact this has been a very costly restoration process that has resulted in the present,

The city remembers the warriors who joined forces to overcome Moslem rule. Here are equestrian statues of El Cid, work of Anna Huntington, protagonist of a brief Christian domination, and of James I, founder of the Kingdom of Valencia, as interpreted by the sculptor Agapito Vallmitjana.

Baroque door of the Cathedral, handsome reredos in stone lifted above an unusual space.

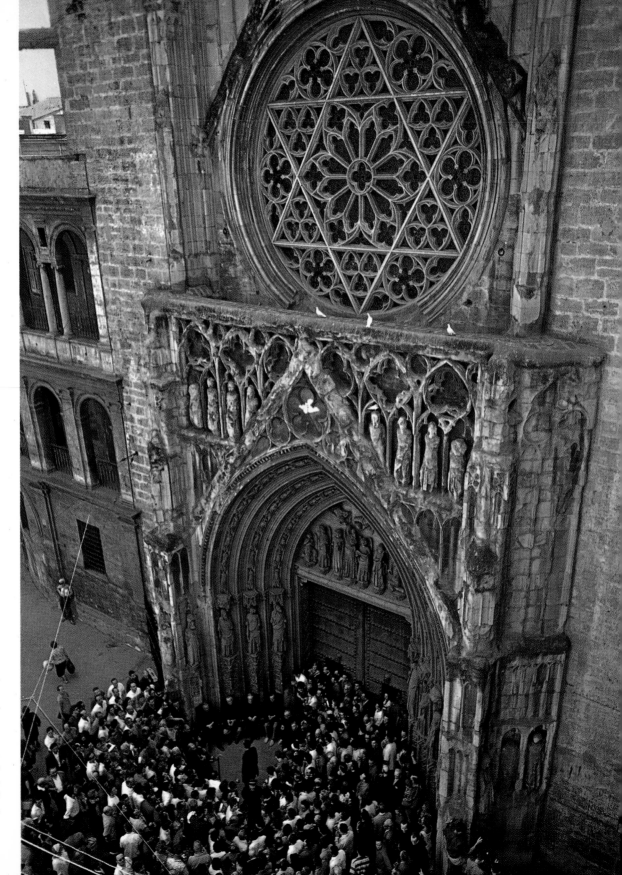

Every Thursday at twelve noon, in front of the Door of the Apostles of the Cathedral, the Tribune of Las Aguas meets, an institution that has its roots in the period preceding the Reconquest.

Museum of the Cathedral. One of the halls of the ground floor in which tablets, sculptures, furniture, books and other objects of historical and artistic interest have been assembled.

Romanesque door of the Cathedral, its contrast with the elements of Gothic design that surround it, enhances its graceful simplicity.

distinctive Gothic form. The exterior of the Cathedral does not present a harmonious configuration. Nonetheless, the three doors, the tower and the dome are well worthy of attention. The very ancient door, which may have been made prior to 1262, is the one of Palau or of l'Almoina. Its style is Romanesque but pertains to Gothic times. Above the archway, halfway down the Cathedral there are magnificent scenes of the Old Testament. The cornice of this archway seems to be supported by fourteen heads. These heads represent the seven married couples who brought to Valencia seventy virgins to be married to the newly-settled Christians. The door of the Apostles was constructed in French Gothic style by Nicholas of Autona at the beginning of the 14th century. Deterioration is extensive and it's in the process of being restored. Every Thursday at twelve o'clock, the Tribunal "de las Aguas de la Vega of Valencia" meets below these arches. Without doubt, this is the oldest institution of justice that exists in Europe, and it deals with lawsuits which arise from the exploitation of the irrigation of the river Turia. A very short, verbal proceeding follows (in the Valencian dialect) and the verdicts handed down cannot be appealed.

The main door, baroque in style,
was initiated by the German architect, Conrado Rodulfo in 1703.
Its style was obviously influenced
by Bernini, and was placed, despite
the difficulties presented by such
a small space, between the tower
and an extraordinary Gothic work
of art. This is a convex-concave
work in stone, with very good
sculptures by Francisco Vergara, "El
Viejo", and Franz Stolff, among
others. The tower, popularly know
as the *Miquelet* or *Miguelete,* has
come to be the symbol of Valencia.
It is octagonal with four sections,
measuring 50.85 m. in height,
equal to the perimeter of its base.
In 1381 it was begun by Andreu
Julia, who was inspired by the bell-
tower, Seo of Lérida. Work was
continued by Pere Balaguer, who
decorated the top section with fine
designs in Gothic style. On the
29th of September, 1418, the day
of Saint Michael, the main bell
was blessed and for this reason the
tower is known by the diminutive
name of the Archangel. The belfry
of the tower was added later, but
not until the 17th century.
Lastly, the dome, which dominates
the external structure of the Cathedral, is an excellent example of
the fine French Gothic style of the
beginning of the 14th century, by
Nicholas of Autona. Once inside
the Cathedral, the first sight to
behold are the restoration works
that are being undertaken to restore

Museum of the Cathedral.
Adoration of the Shepherds,
Renaissance, seemingly of the
Valencian school of the early 16th
century, now attributed to the
Italian Pablo de San Leocadio.

the building to its original Gothic style. The contrast between the old pointed arches and those of neo-classical lines present on the façade which still remains, is very striking. Should we pause for a moment in the Gothic Aula Capitular, which was constructed between 1356 and 1369, we will observe the Flemish clock of the 15th century that has been placed upon the wall. Its Florentine relief work is attributed to Giuliano Poggibonsi, and the Holy Chalice is depicted in a corner of the central part of the vaulted niche. It dates from the 13th century when it was still to be found in the Aragonese monastery of San Juan de la Peña, and it is the same as the one which Christ used to bless the Last Supper. The walls are decorated with the chains once used to close the harbour of Marseilles, broken by the ships of Alphonso V, The Magnanimous, when he took that French city in 1423. From the chapel a side door leads us to the Cathedral Museum. Here, Valencian paintings of the 15th century are exhibited, paintings by Jacomart, Rodrigo of Osona, by the Italianized Vicent Massip and his son, Joan de Joanes, Hernando Yáñez of Almedina, and Hernando

Capitular Room of the Cathedral, before the Theology Room, today chapel of the Holy Chalice. This is in the centre of the flamboyant stone reredos, in which beautiful Renaissance alabaster reliefs by the Florentine, Giuliano Poggibonsi, were placed. The pulpit, seen on the right, similar to the one on the opposite wall, served as a Seat for San Vicente Ferrer, a professor of the school.

The Holy Chalice, revered as is the authentic one that Jesus Christ consecrated on the night of the Last Supper. It is a cup of the Roman epoch on a mounting of the 13th of 14th century.

Llanos, and other fine examples of 17th century Valencian paintings. A visit to the chapel of the "Borja" is a must. Note that the Cathedral of Valencia boasts among its bishops two members of this family: Alonso and Rodrigo of Borja. These figures later became the pontiffs Calixto III and Alexander VI, and the other Borja, Duke of Gandía, who attained sainthood. The chapel is dedicated to him, Saint Francis, and two extraordinary paintings by Goya depict scenes of his life. The one on the right, where we see the saint exorcising an impenitent, is one of the jewels of the religious paintings executed by this brilliant artist from Aragón.

The windows of the Main Altar are worthy of admiration, with twelve large paintings by Yáñez of Almedina and Hernando Llanos. These surround the statue of the Virgin of Portaceli, work of the Valencian sculptor Ignacio Vergara. Beside the presbytery is a pulpit whose Gothic column supports a decorative bowl of precision craftsmanship. According to tradition, San Vicente Ferrer preached Lent sermons from this pulpit in the year 1413. Before leaving the Cathedral, the visitor may pay homage to the remains of several famous people of Valencia. The sepulchrals indicate where each person was buried; here are to be found Ausias March, Gregorio Mayans and Pérez Bayer.

According to tradition, from this pulpit Saint Vicente Ferrer, one of the famous orators of Christianity preached Lent sermons in 1413.

Basilica of the Virgin of the Foresaken and a detail of the vault painted by Antonio Palomino.

THE ROYAL BASILICA OF OUR LADY OF THE FORESAKEN

Alongside the Cathedral is the church that the people of Valencia have dedicated to their patron saint, the *Verge dels Desamparats*. The statue is a beautiful carving of the 15th century, much changed by later restorations and which dominates the chapel from its setting at the Main Altar. The chapel (Basilica is a recent denomination) was built between 1652 and 1667 by Diego Martínez Ponce of Urrama, in a style which might be considered prebaroque. It is oval in shape and the dome above was painted by Antonio Palomino in 1701. The painting is a tremendous glorification of the Virgin. Upon digging the foundations for the temple in 1652, several Roman memorial stones were uncovered. They were found embedded in the main façade. The Palace of the Archbishop was built a quarter of a century ago in front of the Romanesque door of the Cathedral, being the original site that was destroyed in 1936. The very same site was once occupied by the Moorish Alcazar, where "El Cid" established his palace during his short reign over the town.

Following the street "del Palau" to its lowest point, the Palace of the Admirals of Aragon can be seen. The central patio, with its enchanting well and exterior staircase of

Main Altar of the Cathedral presided over by the image of the Virgin. At her feet, children with beautiful voices, who at times sing to her in the Valencian dialect.

*The Virgin of
the Foresaken is
a beautiful
carving of the
15th century,
now in a very
restored state.
The devotion of
Valencia to its
patroness has
recovered its
severe image of
rich shawls and
costly jewels.*

great elegance, is a splendid architectural example of the aristocratic, Mediterranean kingdom of the Crown of Aragón.

Some patios are still preserved in Valencia, a testimony to the splendour of the 15th century. In the Square of Nules, in the street of Caballeros, in one and another narrow street of the mediaeval city, one can catch a glimpse of a beautiful patio, an airy staircase and a tall gallery with delicate columns and handsome arches. Behind the Palace of the Admirals of Aragon are the ancient Arab baths of Moslem tradition: "Abd al-Malik", the only structure remaining in the city pertinent to the period of Moslem domination. Returning to the Cathedral we will contemplate the charming Square of Zaragoza, where the baroque door can be admired, the Miguelete, and the exterior forms of the "Aula Capitular". On the other side the graceful spire reaches towards the heavens. Santa Catalina is a graceful Gothic structure built at the beginning of the 14th century in a severe Cistercian style with three naves. Nearby we come upon the entrance to the street of San Vicente where the church of Saint Martin is to be found.

Valencia conserves some beautiful patios of its old noble houses, which are a testimony to the riches of the city during the 14th and 15th centuries. An example is the Palace of the Admirals of Aragón, reproduced on the following page.

Clear and lucid interior of this temple of the Virgin of the Foresaken. Its present condition, after restoration in the 1940's is due to the architect Vicente Gasco of the 19th century.

El Miguelete, the baroque Door of the Cathedral and the exterior of the Capitular Room serve as a background to the modern Plaza or Square of Zaragoza.

Rococo façade, fantastic and delirious of the Palace of the Marqueses of Dos Aguas, today the National Museum of Ceramics.

THE PALACE OF DOS AGUAS; NATIONAL MUSEUM OF CERAMIC ART

From the street that opens onto the right of the church of Saint Martin, the palace of the Marqueses of Dos Aguas can be reached, where since 1954 the National Museum of Ceramics has been installed; however, beforehand the visitor must admire the splendid bronze sculpture set in a shrine over the door of the church of Saint Martin: the figure of the saint on horseback, a Flemish work dated in 1494 and without a doubt the best sculptural piece conserved in Valencia, considered as one of the major works of universal art. The Palace of Dos Aguas is an example of the most exuberant rococo style. Conceived by the architect Hipólito Rovira, who died insane, it was constructed towards the middle of the 18th century and somewhat retouched in the 19th century. The portal is of alabaster, made by Ignacio Vergara; allusion is made to the title of the Marquis, with its giant atlantes of water flowing from large receptacles borne upon the shoulders of a figure, who ordered the construction of the palace.

The building was extended recently and houses the National Museum of Ceramics, instituted on the basis of a collection belonging to Manuel González Martí, donated to the State by him, on the condition that it should remain in Valencia.

Valencian kitchen, rich and baroque, which has been reconstructed with authentic materials, in the Ceramics Museum. Tablets, tiles, crockery and crafts.

The Museum of Ceramics. Gothic, glazed tile, 14th and 15th century with the fight of Centelles against a dragon.

Museum of Ceramics. Another tile of the 14th or 15th century, in which a boy offers flowers to two damsels.

Museum of Ceramics. Gothic Socarrat with graceful representation of a bull with a highly decorative background.

The interior exemplifies a selection of ceramic works that date from the Iberian epoch until the present. They include pieces from the 13th-15th centuries, encompassing the ceramic work of Paterna and Manises, a collection initiated by the Count of Aranda in 1727 in Alcora, a town with many examples of popular art from the 19th century. Manises is without a doubt the best craftsman known. These ceramic pieces, are accompanied by many works from other Spanish regions. Among others, one can view works representative of Catalunya and Aragón, covering the period from the 16th to the 18th century.

Also to be seen are works from Talavera, Seville and Toledo, and one also witnesses an Italian Renaissance style reflected in the famous *Rondo con la Virgen y el Niño,* attributed to Benedetto of Maiano (15th century), a dinner service typical of the region Maissen (Sajonia), an interesting collection of present-day Swedish ceramics, and four examples of the ceramic art of Picasso. One should not miss the re-construction of the ancient Valencian kitchen; the photograph on pages 28-29 provides an excellent idea of what one will come across when exploring ancient, historical sectors of Valencia. Also exhibited are lovely furnishings, clothing, beautiful fans, sculptures, paintings, drawings, artefacts, all of which relate to an important figure of Valencia. The name of the Museum has been changed to that of The National Ceramic and Sumptuary Industries Museum. Possibly the most interesting item to be found in the second section of the Museum is the carriage pertaining to an important figure, the Marquis of Dos Aguas; it's like the façade of the place, designed and decorated by Hipólito Rovira and executed by Ignacio Vergara.

Museum of Ceramics. Delightful samples of popular ceramics from Manises of the 19th century. The plate and jug form a set, with allusive decorations of the newlyweds who would be gifted with this dishware. In the centre, a monstrance.

Museum of Ceramics. Rondó from the Italian Renaissance of the 15th century, work attributed to Benedetto da Maiano, a follower of Luca della Robbia.

COLLEGE OF THE PATRIARCH

Near the palace of Dos Aguas is the College of Corpus Christi, popularly known as the College of the Patriarch; its founder was San Juan of Ribera, and it is to be noted that he was also the Archbishop and Viceroy of Valencia, as well as patriarch of the city Antioquia, acting as the religious spokesman for the college that is characterized by a pure Trento spirit.

The structure, clearly Italian, was constructed between 1586 and 1610, being a work for the most part of Guillem del Rey; the cloister is today presided over by the sedate, horizontal statue of the patriarch made in 1896 by Benlliure. The temple is decorated profusely with frescoes done by Bartolomé Matarana and other artists; one also is able to view the exceptional *Santa Cena* of Francisco Ribalta which is one of his major works. To the right of the entrance is the Chapel of the Inmaculada that is presided over by a wooden figure probably carved by Gregorio Hernández or at least produced by followers of his school. The walls are adorned with magnificent tapestries of the 16th century from Brussels.

All of the balance and severity of the best Renaissance style is in this patio of the College of Corpus Christi, also called the College of the Patriarch, with its 56 columns of white marble from Genoa. It has been said to be the most elegant cloister of the Spanish Renaissance.

Museum of the College of the Patriarch. Of the three works by El Greco found here, it is this one, Adoration of the Shepherds, *before 1605, that has the greatest artistic merit.*

A thorough search of the Museum reveals a great number of true art treasures, some of which are of exceptional interest, such as the *Tríptico del Calvario* which for many years was attributed to Van der Weyden but which in truth pertains to the Dutch master Thierry Bouts who is one of the best early Flemish painters; three paintings by El Greco: *Alegoría de La Orden Camaldulense,* dated about 1597, *San Francisco and San León meditando sobre la muerte,* and the *Adoracion of the Pastors,* these latter two pertaining to the 17th century; the excellent replica of the *Crucifixión* of *San Pedro* by Caravaggio and paintings by Sariñena, Ribalta, Joanes, and others dating from the 16th-17th century. The leading or most prominent items in the library are some 11,000 volumes reflecting rare, undated manuscripts, original plays by López de Vega, music written by Cabanilles and Comes, composers of Valencia. There exists a large selection of correspondence of Gregorio Mayáns who is an interesting figure of the 18th century. The archives include about 30 thousand documents on file, and more than 2,000 notary manuscripts from the 14th-19th century, and the most complete information concerning the expulsion of the Moslems in 1609.

The chapel of the Purísima of the College of the Patriarch. Towards the rear, an image of the Virgin by Gregorio Hernández or from his school; on the walls, six tapestries from Brussels, a series relating to Vice and Virtue, *of the 16th century.*

*In the Main
Altar of the
church of the
Patriarch, this
Holy Supper by
Francisco
Ribalta can be
viewed, painted
in 1606 and
perhaps his best
work.*

THE UNIVERSITY

In front of the College of the Patriarch and separated from it by a narrow and quiet street called the Nave is to be found the old building of the University, which today is used only as a library, Rector's office and central offices. It was founded by the municipal government and authenticated by Papal Bull of Alexander VI in 1500 and granted royal privilege by Ferdinand the Catholic in 1502. The building, originally of Gothic design, was reformed in 1830 reflecting a neo-classical style replete with a pleasant cloister courtyard in the centre of which is to be found the statue of Juan Luis Vives, the Valencian Humanist who was educated at the University. The main hall reflects the work of Padre Tosca, done in terms of a modern style in 1733; its simple lines are harmonious and boasts a gallery of portraits which includes a wide variety of artistic works depicting prominent figures pertinent to the University. In front of this neo-classical building is the chapel which dates back to 1737; the main altar contains a beautiful virgin figure, *La Virgen de la Sapiencia,* by Nicolás Falcó and executed in 1516.

The old building of the University forms this serene square with the College of the Patriarch. On a wall, a commemorative fountain, installed in 1966, in which are found these statues, by Octavio Vicent of the founders of the University, the Pope Alexander VI and King Ferdinand the Catholic, among other figures.

The library includes books of exceptional merit: *Les trobes en llahors de la Verge Maria,* considered to be the first edition in Spanish (1474), the princely edition of *Tirant lo Blanch* (1490), the exquisite, ancient Codex miniatures, commissioned for the private library of King Alfonso the Magnanimous in Naples, a *Roman de la Rose* with French miniatures of the 14th century, and a Bible that had been gifted by Benedicto XIII to San Vicente Ferrer and which includes a remarkable sign of Byzantine influence.

The University paranymph of classical lines, built in 1733, following plans by P. Tosca, that gives it a severity suitable for academic acts.

THE CONVENT OF SANTO DOMINGO

Alongside of the river, on its right bank and between the Square of Tetuán, is the building of the Military Government in which are to be found elements of the ancient Convent of Santo Domingo, residence of San Vicente Ferrer. With the help of a well-planned restoration programme initiated in 1956 at the expense of the military authorities, one can today admire the attractive cloister and the chapel hall exemplary Gothic structures; here are preserved arches of the second half of the XIV century together with other artistic accomplishment of that period. The chapel hall is one of the most beautiful that remains of Spanish Gothic style dating from the 13th century with four tall, graceful columns of stone that seem to open out like a palm tree, forming the bulwark of the arched roof that served to inspire the designer of the House of Commerce of Palma and Valencia. The tomb of the family of Pere Boil is set in one of the walls; it was he who financed the construction of the lecture hall. The king's chapel its vault without ribs, exposes its structure, pertaining to the second third of the 15th century. Here is to be found the tomb of the Marquis of Zenete. The façade of the convent is done in a Renaissance style It is said to be designed by Philip II when he visited Valencia en 1858.

Two views of the eastern gallery of the cloister of the church of Santo Domingo, unique with arches with traceries, two of them from the 13th century; of French Gothic style are the rest.

Façade of the convent of Santo Domingo, in Castillian, Renaissance style; it is said to have been planned by Falipe II during his visit to Valencia in 1585.

THE WALLS

Valencia was a city enclosed within walls until 1865. They remained intact until that date, having been constructed in 1365, later enlarged upon to encompass the growing urban community; the oldest part corresponds to the door of Valldigna, built in 1400.

The passage afforded by the Caldererìa is one of the few ancient remains that are to be found today. From the ruins torn down in 186. the only elements that have been salvaged are the Door of Los Serranos and the Door of the Quart. The Door of the Serranos, better known as the *Torres dels Serrans* was constructed between 1392 and 1398 by Pere Balaguer. Inspired in the *Porta Reial,* of the Monastery of Poblet, but superior to the original model, being one of the best examples of Gothic military architecture known in Europe. Made entirely of stone it affords a sensation of strength and grace by virtue of the harmony of its proportions and its rich ornamentation, akin to an Arch of Triumph rather than an imposing defensive structure. The Door of Quart was at one time the main entrance to Valencia from the West. It was constructed between 1441 1460, half a century later than that of Serranos, by Pere Bonfill and inspired by the Castel Nuovo of Naples. Made of stone and morter devoid of lavish ornamentation, it is certainly to be admired as a magnificent fortification.

The well in the house where San Vicente Ferrer was born, its water, famous for working miracles, is fervently drunk by many Valencians.

The door of Valldigna was opened in 1440 in the wall, as an access to the Arabian Quarter.

NOSTRA·DONA
DE·LA·BONA·SON
PRESVEV·PER·NOS
PORTAL
DE·VALLDIGNA

Another reminder of the old walled part of mediaeval Valencia is the Puerta de Quart — Torres de Quart — a work by Pere Bonfill, around the beginning of the 15th century.

MUSEUMS OF PRE-HISTORY AND PALEONTOLOGY

In the palace of the Bailía, in the Square of Manises, in front of the Generalidad, is to be found the Museum of Pre-History, operated under the auspices of the township and directly related to services pertaining to pre-historical investigations; it was founded in 1927 by Isidro Ballester. The Museum includes a wide variety of materials that afford a well-balanced perspective of the chronological developments relating to the history of Valencia. One of the few testimonies known in Spain of the Neanderthal Man can be viewed; also available for inspection are limestone plaques; receptacles representative of the Neolithical period, being true art treasures of their kind, with interesting decorations, a wide assortment of remains that have been found buried collectively in small caves, corresponding to the Eneolithic period and others, and many items derived from numerous villages that pertain to the Age of Bronze, and various Iberian settlements dating between IV and I B.C.; all are of high artistic and historical merit; the ceramic vessels to be seen are decorated with unique forms of movement and design. They depict interesting primitive scenes of tribal wars as well as

There are very few remains of the Neanderthal Man known in Spain. One of them, a Skull, found near Játiva, in the Prehistoric Museum.

In the old Almudín the Museum of Paleontology is to be found, with an excepcional array of vertebrated fossils, like the Megatherium, in the main hall.

This warrior in bronze, of the 4th century B.C., was found in the Iberian town of La Bastida de les Alcuses *and is one of the best pieces that the Museum of Prehistory keeps.*

scenes of conflict between sea-going vessels, and lastly, the domestication of animals. These items come from the Cerro of San Miguel de Liria. The Museum is also rich in Iberian inscriptions and in stone sculptures dating back to the IV B.C. Not far away is to be found the Paleontological Museum instituted on the basis of funds brought from South America by José Rodrigo Botet that he gifted to Valencia. It contains the most important collection of vertebrate fossils relative to Southamerican land animals that exists in Europe; to be admired is the skeleton of a megathere, a giant *Eutatus* and abundant cuirasses or armor plating from glyptodonts. If the paleontological collection is of singular importance, not less interesting is the building that houses it, constructed in the 14th century to serve as a deposit for grains, it was reformed and extended in 1517 wherein its primitive and typical layout characteristic of a Roman basilica was preserved, consisting of a rectangular area with a central nave, used originally for conducting business, and a cloister with half-point arches, among which is one of Byzantine characteristics, used for storing the grains.

Iberian ceramic art reached its maximum expression in this vase, of the 2nd century B.C., found in Cerro de San Miguel de Liria and on display in the Museum of Prehistory.

PALACE OF THE COMMUNITY

Next to the small garden that takes us to the Square of the Virgin, which was the Roman and medieval city, is the Palace of The Community, where today is located the Provincial Townhall. It is an indirect tribute to the city, administrated by the estates —*braços*— of the Kingdom, that came to be a representative authority of the Court. The work was begun in 1482, directed by Pere Compte; the central section was the focal point of this effort that was later completed in 1510 by Joan Corbera and Joan Montano. This latter figure had responsibility for constructing the tower to the right, begun in 1518 in a sort of hybrid style reflecting Doric and Renaissance elements and culminated in 1585 with a vignette. The hefty tower that overlooks the street of Serranos was erected in accordance with old blueprints between 1940 and 1952.

Entering from the street of Caballeros one proceeds on to the patio, stately and typical of Gothic structures found in Valencia. To the right is to be found the *Sala Dorada,* or gilted room, with splendid works of craftsmanship (1534-1575), designed by Ginés Linares and gilted by Joan Cardona and others, representing one of the marvels of Valencian artisanry of the 16th century. Adjoining this room

The palace of the Generalidad. In this room, called the Salón de Cortes, the provincial council now meets.

is another smaller one also with a less lavish finish, a work by Linares and completed by his son Pedro and painted and gilted by Luis Mata, their efforts being made between 1535 and 1583.

From the patio, using an attractive Gothic staircase, it is possible to go up to the first floor, which is today called the *Salón de Reyes* owing to the series of portraits of kings of Valencia that are to be found there; previously called the *Oratorio*, where there is preserved still a magnificent altarpiece (1606-1607) with paintings by Sariñena. Herein we find the *Salón de Cortes,* one of the most interesting rooms of the 17th century in Spain. It has been given this name because the four *braços* or estates of the Valencian Court and the Township of the Kingdom are represented in a series of pictures that cover the walls, paintings by Sariñena, Requena and others, done between 1591 and 1593. The panelled ceiling and gallery are of more category, non-gilted wood and unpainted, a work of Ginés Linares (1540), and of Gaspar Gregori, carved between the years 1563 and 1566.

View of the patio — one of the most beautiful of Valencia, of the Palace of the Generalidad. It is partly a work of Pere Compte, who also built the House of Commerce. The patio that we see was begun in 1482.

The Sala Dorada, in the Palace of the Generalidad, with rich panels of the 16th century, now decorated with tapestries, pictures, and furniture, is one of the best rooms left of the Spanish Renaissance.

THE CENTRAL MARKET PLACE

One of the vital centers of Valencia was the market place where important events concerning the city took place. Today there are no longer tent-like structures and stalls, being substituted by the imposing building of the Central Market, one of the most luxurious in Europe in its day and the building of most important modernist tendencies in Valencia. It was constructed during the years 1910 and 1928, in accordance with a project put forth by the architects Guardia Vidal and Soler March of Barcelona.

The Central Market, huge building of cement and iron, presents this interior view, of a stream of colours.

THE HOUSE OF COMMERCE AND THE MARITIME CONSULATE

In front of the Market is the House of Commerce and the Maritime Consulate. The House of Commerce is one of the best civil Gothic buildings in all of Europe. Pere Compte, helped by Joan Iborra, built the hall divided into three naves by eight fine, eleven meter high helicoidal columns forming the nerves of the arched roof whose keystones are 17 m. above the floor. Inspired, Pere Compte excelled the model in grandeur and beauty in the House of Commerce of Palma de Mallorca, adorning windows and doors with vivid ornaments and with graceful sculptures and numerous gargoyles and details.

The House of Commerce is still used for trading today.

The Maritime Consulate was built behind the House of Commerce. Construction started in 1506 and finished in 1584; it is still of Gothic style but full of beautiful, Italian-type decorations, of clear Renaissance influence, noticeable especially in the high gallery.

The Maritime Consulate and the House of Commerce form a delightful corner with a garden, evoking the Valencia of the early sixteenth century when it rivalled Seville for the honour of being the most beautiful city in Spain. As many Mediterranean cities, Valencia continues to produce great works of Art.

The House of Commerce, door of access to the Maritime Consulate, done in a beautiful flamboyant Gothic style.

Golden and polychromed panelled ceiling — crimson, green, black and gold on a blue base — which, coming from the Town Hall, destroyed by a fire, was moved to the Main Hall of the Maritime Consulate.

The immense columned hall of the House of Commerce, a marvel of universal, civil, Gothic architecture, continues to be used today, as in medieval times, for commerce.

*he House of Commerce and the Maritime
*onsulate are the most important
*onumental group in Valencia. The
*ifference in styles between both buildings
mbines so well that it forms one unit.

*he Church of Santos Juanes, where we
*e its baroque, rear façade facing the
*ustere House of Commerce, next to the
Market.

CHURCH OF SANTOS JUANES

In front of the House of Commerce and almost next to the Central Market is the Church of Santos Juanes, known in Valencia as *Sant Joan del Mercat*. Although built in 1368 it was totally transformed in the early 18th century, following the Italian baroque style, of which the near wall is an example. Its interior, very ornate but forming a unity with its rich decoration, has a dome painted by Antonio Palomino, his best work according to art historians.

THE TOWN HALL

The city life is today centered in the Square of the Caudillo.

It is spacious, light and lively at all hours. Here are the Palace of Communications, the telephone exchange, Ateneo, commercial banks, shoppes, pubs, and the Town Hall. It has been occupied since 1859, before, the site of an old school house, that has been changed and enlarged during the years. The façade has sculptures by Beltrán, Benlliure and Carmelo Vicent; it was completed in 1928. In it there is an exceptional wealth of documents of the city; the Archives contain documents from 1301, and what is more, there are many works of historical and artistic interest.

One can see the Tablets of the Last Judgement, 15th century. Paintings by Espinosa, Vicente López, Sorolla, Muñoz Degrain and unique manuscripts, *Furs*, of Valencia 1329, *Llibre del Consolat del Mar* (1409). The Iberian treasures were found in the village of Cheste; the Roman mosaic found in the old center of Valencia; the Pendón of the Conquest, the *Senyera* of the city, a sword of James I, reputedly belonging to him. The important map of Valencia sketched by P. Tosca in 1703, and many other testimonies alluding to the past of the city; to contemplate them is to embark upon a journey through its history.

The administrative centre of the city, the Town Hall, is in the heart of modern Valencia, in the Square of the Caudillo.

The Hall of Acts of the Town Hall. ▷

The Senyera of the city — flag of Valencia — which is kept in the Municipal Archives.

The only example of the Llibre del Consolat del Mar, *codex of 1409, one of the treasures of the Municipal Archives.*

THE GLORIETA AND THE PALACE OF JUSTICE

It is said, *For beautiful gardens, go to Valencia,* and this typical phrase is completed with, *Valencia, land of flowers.*

Without a doubt this is quite true; the Garden Real or Royal Garden, La Alameda, a poplar grove, La Glorieta, El Parterre, Monforte garden, and other small, natural corners, and all of which represented a large part of the city when it was five to six times smaller. Moreover, orchards were cultivated as though they were gardens and they began where the city ended, and of course this is why it was said, "Valencia, land of the beautiful flowers".

Todays city growth has pushed the beautiful orchards farther and farther away. The gardens are still preserved, perhaps more so, but they are scattered through out the large mass of new buildings. A few corners remain, in secluded parts of the present city, in which it is still possible to walk leisurely and peacefully. One of these places is the Glorieta, with the Parterre alongside, forming a peaceful walkway through the major part of the city. The first trees were planted in 1813, supervised by French General Suchet, and the garden was improved upon a few years later by General

Elio, who ordered the installation of the magnificent Tritón fountain, of the most pure Italian rococo style by Giacomo Ponzanelli, dating from 1700.

Next to the Glorieta, is the Parterre park of trees, where the visitor can admire the handsome statue of James I, conqueror of Valencia; it is an excellent work in bronze by the sculptor Vallmitjana, done in 1891. At the angle formed by the Parterre and the Glorieta, is the actual Palace of Justice, one of the most handsome buildings of Valencia. It is rectangular, simple, perfectly balanced, with lines and proportions of precision. It was built between the years 1768 and 1802, according to plans by Antonio Gilabert and Felipe Rubio, within the neo-classical style, but reducing the stark features by the balustrade that is on the Architrave, with the shield of Charles III in relief, on the façade with a group of sculptures that concluded in what represents the king and two allegoric figures of Justice and the other, Prudence, executed by Ignacio Vergara. The interior of the Palace conserves the dignity of the central court and the noble stairs leading to the upper floor.

Through the years it has suffered many modifications until it has come to take on its present configuration and function as the Palace of Justice.

Present building of the Court House. Of severe, harmonic, neo-classical style, it wa. built in the second half of the 18th century for use by Customs, then changed to a tobacco factory until, in 1922, it became the seat of the Tribune of Justice.

LA ALAMEDA

In the centre of the large oval square which is next to the Glorieta, a neo-classical gate was built in 1946, with the Cross of the Fallen under its main arch. The gate is an exact replica of that of the Real, one of those which gave access to the city at the start of the 19th century.

From here the visitor can cross the river Turia and get to the Alameda, the most noble of the Valencian walks, by any of the nearby bridges. Limited by two fountains, one at each end, it has a wide central road and two lateral pavements with abundant trees that allow the passers-by enjoy a fresh and peaceful stroll. For this reason it has been the favourite promenade of the Valencians since the 16th century, when it was still called El Prado, until about 50 years ago.

It was given its present configuration at the end of the 18th century, and its name, Alameda, was provided in 1645, when many trees were planted, especially poplars. In its first part, nearest to the Royal Gardens, two graceful turrets were built for the keepers in 1714.

Royal Gardens among the trees, flowers and shady walks, where there are comforting waterfalls that provide a pleasant spot for relaxing and momentarily forgetting about the bustle of life in a large, populous city.

MUSEUM OF FINE ARTS

The building of Saint Pío V, of beautiful and airy baroque style, was built in 1683 by Juan Bautista Pérez for a clergyman's college. Afther its disentailment and until 1941 when the Provincial Museum of Fine Arts started to be installed there, it passed through many hands with unsuitable results. Today an extraordinary picture gallery, a good sculpture collection and some archeological pieces of great interest are kept there. The initial nucleus of its treasures is represented by the collection of the Royal Academy of St. Charles, where other works came as a consequence of the disentailment and from donations and legacies; the pictures by Goya, Ribera, Velázquez, the best of Joanes and many others, were obtained in this way.

The most interesting series that can be admired is, without a doubt, that formed by the works of the old Valencians: altarpieces by the Syndicate of Carpenters and the very famous work by Fray Bonifacio Ferrer, works by Marçal de Sax, Pedro Nicolau, Lorenzo Zaragoza, Gonzalo Pérez, Maestros de Perea and Juan Sivera, all between the middle of the 14th and the end of the 15th centuries, and with them those of the 16th century: Nicolás Falcó, both Osona the Master of Artés and of El Grifo, some already bordering on the beginning of the Renaissance period.

Museum of Fine Arts. The richness in primitive Valencian art is evident in this hall; the altarpiece of the Three Kings by Maestro de Perea and at the end, the altarpiece of Purity with carvings by Damian Forment.

Museum of Fine Arts. This self-portrait of Velázquez is, apart from Las Meninas, the most authentic of the painter.

*Museum of Fin
Arts. Altarpie
of the Holy
Cross, beginnin
of the 15th
century,
attributed to
Miguel Alcañ*

*Museum of Fin
Arts. Famous
altarpiece by
Fray Bonifaci
Ferrer, untitled
an excellent
example of the
Toscan influen
in Valencian a
of the end of th
14th century.*

Museum of Fine Arts. Goya, 1795, portrayed Lady Joaquina Candado — who accompanied him to Valencia as head-servant, and made a landscape of the Albufera as a background for the painting.

*Museum of Fine Arts. Sorolla's picture
of youth, his fabulous form of
interpretation of the light of Valencia.*

The visitor must not forget to admire the Renaissance collection of Hernando de Llanos and Hernando Yáñez of Almedina, scholars and devote disciples of Leonardo, of Joan de Joanes, of the Ribalta brothers and other examples of Valencian schools dating from the 17th to the 18th century. Naturally the splendid series of the 19th and 20th centuries, pertaining to Vicente López, a friend and disciple of Goya, and up to the corresponding non-figurative artists including Domingo Marqués, Pinazo, Sorolla, the Benlliure, also Muñoz Degrain, Lozano, and many other artists of merit. Those artists of special merit are classified and are found in a section apart: *Self-portrait* of the gifted Velázquez, *San Juan Bautista* by El Greco, *San Sebastián* by Ribalta, the portrait, *Retrato del Marqués de Aytona* by Van

Of the two tablets of Joan of Joanes depicting El Salvador—in one, blond, and in the other, dark—exhibited in the Museum of Fine Arts; here we see the "dark" one, that carries the Holy Chalice in its left hand.

Dick, the splendid series of portraits by Goya, a painting of Morales, of Murillo, a very good selection of Italian works. The sculpture section forms a minor part, with a separate section pertaining to archeology and for this it has formed a distinct group in the museum that includes interesting Gothic pieces from the Renaissance, and baroque reliefs, a sarcophagus, images, tombstones and sculptures by Capuz and by Inurria.

Also Benlliure, whose works are presented in various halls, magnificent themes of his life, and of the famous model, the monumental tomb of Joselito, and finally the important collection of a few archeological items that are of world repute, such as works as *León* of Bocairente, extraordinary Iberian sculptures of the 4th century B.C., and Latin-incribed stones.

A good collection of descriptive sculpture, mosaics and Roman painted ceramics, and one sarcophagus of the Constantinian era, with simple ornamentation in low relief, that for many years was considered not to be a part of any of the two classifications—devoid of archeological or historical content, like that used for the burial of San Vicente Mártir.

Of the Valencian Jacomart, of the first hald of the 15th century, the Museum of Fine Arts, only keeps this fine tablet of Saint James and Saint Gil Abad.

One of the most well-known works by Mariano Benlliure is the Mausoleum of the bullfighter, José el Gallo, "Joselito". The museum has the original in plaster.

OTHER ASPECTS OF VALENCIA

Among the figures who enjoyed fame in life, the city has not forgotten three, a painter—Sorolla—, a novelist—Blasco Ibáñez—, and a musician—Serrano. To the last, a few years ago this gracious monument, work of Octavio Vicent, was erected in a central spot of Valencia.

Up to now we have only taken the visitor through one part of the city, that part of Valencia where, each two steps, is to be found a monument, a church, a silent witness to the past; at times we are taken past a new building, modern, of bold lines. But the visitor has hardly left what was the old part of the city, the Valencia that, until 1865, was enclosed within the old walls. There are still many things one could consider: Other churches, other corners with lingering memories, other testimonies of its history. But Valencia is something more than this. It is a city in continual demographic and territorial expansion; it has over 640,000 inhabitants and an area of over 20 square kilometers. It is, as the reader will hear said so many times, the third capital of Spain.

We are going to go into the new town, *el ensanche,* perhaps rather impersonal, but with wide streets, spacious walks and clear perspectives. Even more, considering its uniformity, you can find beautiful walks, agreeable corners, and buildings worthy of being admired. Thus the reader must follow us along the Gran Vía del Marqués del Turia; on both sides he will

be able to see some samples of the always interesting *modernist* architecture, alternating with buildings of the most recent tendencies, and also the beautiful monuments, work of Mariano Benlliure, erected in 1909 in honour of the Marquis of Campo, one of the most interesting figures of Valencia in the second half of the 19th century. Forming an angle with the Gran Vía is a delightful avenue, that of José Antonio, with its central promenade adorned with palm trees and bordered by hedges; here is the gracious monument to Maestro Serrano, the most popular of the Valencian composers, a work by Octavio Vicent and, a little farther on, the fantastic façade of the Colegiata de San Bartolomé, by Cillero, one of the most daring and interesting urban monuments of current religious architecture. Passing to the other side of the river and after crossing the Alameda, is the widest Valencian promenade, El Paseo al Mar, which, starting in the Royal Gardens, reaches the beach between the Cabanyal and the Malvarrosa, where it ends; it is 100 meters wide and buildings of the city's university are to be found here, Schools of Medicine and Science, already quite old, and Schools of Law and Fine Arts, very modern, which flank the promenade.

In the Paseo al Mar, year after year, the modern buildings of the new University are being built. Here we see the Faculty of Law, of simple lines, functional, the work of the architect Fernando Moreno Barberá, opened in 1963.

Returning by the Paseo to the sea we find the Royal Gardens, also known as Viveros Municipales. They are, without a doubt, the most extensive and popular gardens of the city, a place of childrens' playgrounds, a quiet spot, and excellent for relaxing strolls. And they are also the oldest gardens; it seems that in Arabian times the King of Valencia, Abd al-Aziz, installed his *almunia* here in the middle of the 11th century, a park the Christian kings later took advantage of to build the royal palace that, with modifications and reconstructions, lasted until 1811 when it was completely destroyed. It is said that king John I, at the end of the 14th century, started a kind of zoological park with lions, camels, bears, gazelles and other exotic animals. Today the Royal Gardens have, among its flowers and trees, a childrens' park, a small but interesting zoo, a restaurant and a series of places for concerts and theatre performances, that in the hot summer nights, in the open air, are certainly pleasant.

From the Royal Gardens the visitor can continue his stroll through many places of the city; in all he will find a pleasant atmosphere since Valencia continues to be a happy city.

The priceless documents of the Archive of the Kingdom which were in a precarious state for many years, today are kept in a magnificent building by the architect Juan Segura de Lagos, which is alongside of the Alameda.

In the Royal Gardens, doors and other elements of an architectonic nature have been gathered together, derived from torn-down palaces, estates, and churches; these elements, placed in this lush green setting, enhace the beauty of the gardens. This is apparent from the partial view offered here above; below, to the left, the door of the church of the Convent of San Julián and, to the right, that of the palace of the Duke of Mandas.

VALENCIA AND THE SEA

About three miles from the urban centre of Valencia, is found the sea, whose waters caress an extensive beach of fine golden sand. From it extends the Maritime District: in the centre the Grao—the Vila Nova of the Sea, or, as it is also called, the Grau of the Sea—; to the north, the Canyamelar, the Cabanyal and the Cap de França, all little old fishing towns, which, before being linked to the Grao and thereby becoming a district of the capital, formed the municipality of the Poble Nou of the Sea; and, to the south, Nazaret, next to the mouth of the river Turia. Medieval Valencia, by ist essentially sea-faring character, looked to the waters of the Mediterranean for ist expansion and, by means of this sea, found richness and prosperity. The importance of the high medieval, maritime, mercantile traffic of Valencia can be deduced from the establishment there, in 1283, and therefore, before Barcelona and Palma, of the celebrated tribunal of the *Consolat del Mar*. Little remains of the sailing splendour of Valencia since of the port we only hear tales of simple wooden piers, re-built so many times, and of the promenades constructed in 1338 and renovated in 1500, there remain only five very disfigured, beautiful Gothic pointed arches of great width and height

The excellent temperature that Valencians enjoy permits them to take pleasure in the sun and water during many months of the year. The Nautical Club, next to the port, with its attractive pool.

Shipbuilding has a long tradition in Valencia, represented today by an important industry located between the port and the river Turia. Here, ships of great size are made for a world market. The port is situated on a flat and sandy beach with poor and shallow waters. Next to the mouth of the river Turia is an example of the tenacious spirit of the Valencians who, at the end of the 18th century, continued to build with wood that was perpetually exposed to the action of the river Turia. In 1865 began the construction of a stone pier that was destroyed by strong storms before it was completed, but not until the middle of the 19th century was the foundation permanently set and at the same time it was also repaired, perhaps insufficiently for the needs of Valencia, which is the centre of exportation for agricultural products. Activity and transit during the export period for oranges is undescrible with its mass movement and bustle.

One can frequently see, away from the mouth of the port, various ships, waiting at a dock to be loaded.

The fishing boats, motors at rest and the nets drying on the mast, moving in the serene port, between two sea journeys.

Fishermen, sailors, dock-workers, etc. seem to form a composite brigade. All of them blend together with their special skills, adding a special touch of grace to the district of Valencia which belongs and participates in different facets of the economic growth of the city.

As we accompany the visitor to the port, we give a glimpse at the Royal staircase; we then proceed down many steps until we arrive near the edge where we can almost touch the water with the palm of our hand. Hopefully, if it is a splendid day, it will be possible to take a cruise in a launch to the port. The motor boat that makes tours is anchored next to the Royal staircase. If we continue our journey from here to the right after returning from the dock, we reach the Paseo del Caro, where we can see the simple white building of the Nautical Club in front where anchored to the dock are numerous boats of private sport, and seagulls perch upon the water. If the visitor wants to have a view of the entire port, he can catch a glimpse from the piers of the Cabanyal and the Caballeros.

The beach of Nazaret, owing to its magnificent attractions—soft sand, calm waters and shallowness, near as well to the centre of the city—is always a favourite spot for most people.

LA HUERTA

La Huerta is an expanse of irrigated land covered by fruit trees; it is a natural part of the city and of course Valencia is the capital. This region extends from North to South, from Puzol to Catarroja, almost until reaching Albufera, and East and West, from the beaches to Manises, about thirty kilometers long and about ten kilometers wide, characterized by flat, fertile green land that is productive throughout the year. It is dotted with a thousand colours. The land is irrigated by eight different irrigation ditches. Every Thrusday at twelve noon the cultivators benefiting from the irrigation system meet at the Door of the Apostles of the Cathedral to discuss various problems and projects. "...the beauty of the Huerta is a tradition; it's like standing in a. cultivated primrose garden," extending for more than 400 kilometers. A beautiful sight to walk through. It continues where Valencia ends. Every day there are fewer quaint shacks, but our guide continues to find typical ones with rectangular configurations, walls of clay always whitewasthed, slanting roofs made of straw. The orchards include arbors, palm trees, other fruit trees, that complete part of its charm.

Typical dress of the workers in the orchards, lavish and baroque for the woman, still worn today by children and young people in traditional Valencian festivals.

LA ALBUFERA

It's a fresh water lake to the south of Valencia that joins with the sea. It has a long strip of sand that is named the Dehesa and is separated by the Mediterranean. Along the shore there's an important urbanization, between a pine grove. Hotels, sports' grounds, and many individual attractions are available to the visitor. It is easy to cross to the lake, which is very close to the city. The sunset, a lovely time to cross it, in a boat gliding on the calm water, catching the wind with billowing sails, an unforgettable moment of green shores and sparkling blue waters, especially in the center, *el Lluent,* where there's a calm and peaceful sailing, like on a cloud. The scenery is gloriously described by the novelist Blasco Ibáñez in *Cañas y barro.* One must visit the island of El Palmar, the scene of the novel, remniscent of boats, fishermen, of windswept beauty touched by the author. Fishing and game hunting are two of the important activities of La Albufera. Professional fishing and hunting are a hobby. There are aquatic birds; there are usually about twenty shoots between September and March.

These shoots, called *Les Tirades,* are famous among hunters from all over Spain. As regards fishing, the eels are considered to be of good quality.

Cañas y barro *is the title of one of the most famous novels by Blasco Ibáñez. The narrative revolves about Albufera, seen here, and the tiny island—now joined to the edge of the lake—of El Palmar.*

The Barraca, *typical housing found in the region of the orchards, exhibiting their clean whiteness and pureness of lines among the villages, always green in the suburbs.*

At present La Albufera covers some three thousand hectares, when in Roman times it is said to have covered thirty-thousand. This great waste of land is partly due to natural causes, however, in another sense it is due to the clandestine efforts of the workers of the neighbouring communities that, with an exemplary tenacity, fill the ground with soil, transforming the lake into productive rice fields. With the regulation of drainage to the sea, using sluice-gates, the nutrious water is held back and keeps the level of the water necessary for each stage of the rice cultivation.

FIESTAS IN VALENCIA

The Valencian calendar is full of *fiestas*. Important *fiestas* that the entire town celebrates, *fiestas* of less category that affect a district, small *fiestas* that affect only the neighbours of a street, members of a society or brotherhood, and even private *fiestas* — a wedding, a baptism — have an external expression, usually celebrated with fireworks and bonfires; those who are celebrating want everyone to participate in their joy, and join them in the noise and excitement.

Between the months of September and October, the land around Albufera presents this animated aspect: the harvesting of the rice crop.

The great Valencian *fiestas* are becoming fewer and almost disappearing. Some because of their inappropriateness in modern times, others, religious ones, due to changes introduced into the liturgy and also due to social-psychological transformations. The popular *fiestas* remaining are the *Fallas,* July and Christmas fairs, this latter most certainly accepted by the children and common folk. The religious festivals, reduced to a few austere and devoted celebrations, have lost a great part of their popularity and only take place among fervent worshippers; the day dedicated to the Virgin of the Foresaken—the second Sunday of May—remains, with its crowded and noisy procession, a demonstration of a simple and popular fervour; some details of the pre-baroque and colourful procession of Corpus Christi; the *fiesta* of *Els Gloriosos,* at midnight of the Saturday of the Resurrection.

The famous oranges and traditional costumes of the workers in the orchards. They are two elements that, together with the Valencian paella, *are more than sufficient to characterize the Valencian region.*

And *Els Miracles,* scenes of life, often of the legend by San Vicente Ferrer, acted out by children in Valencian dialect, on stages set in a baroque style made of wood, installed in distinct sections of the city that are permanent. The visitor who finds himself in Valencia on the Sunday and Monday following the Easter Sunday must look for an *altar;* some are to be found in the Square of the Virgin, street of the Mar, in front of the church of Santos Juanes, facing the House of Commerce, and in three or four other points of Valencia; it is of interest to study this curious demonstration of the cult which the proud city of Valencia dedicates to San Vicente Ferrer, the saint who was born in this city and who is so affectionately and actively loved by its people. Visitors are sure to find these *fiestas* strange and extremely interesting traditions that are probably unfamiliar to him.

Several months in advance of March, many craftsmen of the city invest their best efforts in the preparations for the Fallas. The workshops dedicated to this activity are like the one shown here, in a fairly advanced stage in the construction of a Falla.

Predominant characteristics of all Valencian *fiestas* are the noise and fireworks, along with the participation of all of the town, so that the *fiesta* penetrates right into the most hidden corners of the city.

All through the *Week of the Fallas,* which takes place in March during the week before the day of San José, on the 19th, and ends at midnight of that day, the city is one continual explosion. An explosion of light and sun, of colour, augmented by those monuments of cardboard and wood that are called *Fallas,* by the typical dresses worn by the innumerable girls bearing flags—four red stripes on a yellow background edged by a blue bar—which abound everywhere; of music, since around a hundred bands walk through the town streets from one end to the other; and noise to which an uninterrupted firing of rockets and other artefacts' sounds contribute. It all reaches a glorious, extravagently, colourful grand climax at the hour of midnight of the nineteenth of March, the day of San José, when one hundred and fifty or more *fallas* blaze in a furious thunder that is without equal among the multicolour arabesks that form the castles of the fireworks in the sky and among the sounds, some already so far out of tune after so many days of riotous hilarity and *fiesta,* of the music of the bands.

Valencians are characterized by fire and noise. Both elements combine perfectly in the beautiful castles of fireworks that explode noisily and colourfully throughout the festival.

View of the Square of Zaragoza, heart of Valencian life and also the centre of the principal acts of the festival of the Fallas.

The *falla* is a shed made of wood and cardboard, with a type of platform on which there is a series of groups of figures, more or less caricaturesque — *minots* — representing scenes in a satirical fashion. Nowadays, the *fallas,* sometimes constructed by famous sculptors, have reached a rare perfection: its daring architecture, the quality of their figures converts them into ephemeral works of art which are maliciously critical. Aside from the possible relationship of the fires with very old rites of fire cults, and ceremonies relating to the equinox of spring, an antecedent has been found in the 16th century, in the custom of the carpenters, of burning, on the eve of the feast of St. Joseph, the patron of the trade, the supports of the oil lamps, and other forms of illumination, now unnecessary as the day lengthens. Then they would go on to add shavings and useless pieces of wood, old furniture, and rags. Later they would make images from them: in the 18th century, they had very well-made groups of figures, but until the end of the last century they did not reach the form, which, with more or less modifications, has now reached our times. At the *fiesta* of the *fallas* proper, complementary acts and spectacles have been added, which has increased its interest: among them, the Offering of Flowers to the Virgin, the Cabalgata of the Ninot and the bullfights.

The young people of the committees of all of the Fallas *offer flowers to the Patroness of the city. The façade of the Basilica presents a marvellous aspect in which the colours blend with the perfumed air.*

The Feria of July, which is celebrated during the second fortnight of this month, is now the event which follows the *fiesta* of the *fallas* in importance and popular acceptance. Created by the Town Council in 1870 in order to delay the summer exodus and favour the local business, wine being, till the Twenties, the principal Valencian entertainment. The wide and beautiful Paseo de la Alameda becomes the heart of the fair, and on it are installed strongly lit baroque pavilions, in which there is dancing till very late every night, generally, till after the castle of fireworks has been displayed, which, towards midnight, fills the sky with multicoloured stars.

The visitor has the opportunity of watching the nine or more bullfighters with programmes which bring together the best bullfights, of the time; he can also watch the floral displays, or the musical and theatrical events which are celebrated in the Jardines del Real, but he must not miss the flower battle, the animated and beautiful spectacle, with which the July Fair ends.

The participation of the Valencians in the festival of the Fallas *is absolute. It is impossible to avoid them. The children, as soon as they can walk, take part in the festivities and so assure the future of the* Fallas.

Paella, the festival dish of Valencian cooking, has, on its own merits, grown to be internationally famous and today is served in all restaurants of the world. But to know what a real paella tastes like it's necessary to try it in Valencia.

VALENCIAN GASTRONOMY

The reader, native or foreign, from near or far, on hearing of gastronomy will immediately have thought, we are sure, of Paella. The rice in Paella, which is how it must be described since the *paella* is the flatbottomed shallow frying pan without a handle in which the rice is cooked, enjoys such a renown that it is undoubtedly the most internationally known dish of Spanish cooking. Notoriety has not favoured it, since any cook believes he can make it by following a recipe and ignoring the fact that the quality of this dish does not depend on its ingredients which vary according to the time of year and the part of Valencia in which it is cooked, but in having the knack of preparing the rice in order that each grain falls away and that is neither too hard or too soft. The visitor, can verify the difference which exists between the paella which is made in Valencia and that which is from outwith our region. Paella can be chicken, with a little pork or fish and shellfish, or also, a mixture, with chicken and fish.

We would recommend that the reader does not neglect to try other rice dishes and, perhaps, among them, none better than the *rosejat,* cooked in the oven in an earthenware dish, with chick peas, sausage and pork, which is a treat for the palate.

But Valencian cooking does not only have rice dishes. There is a wide tasty variety, and in general, with a baroque appearance. The visitor who moves to the Albufera must try a dish which can only be found there cooked as it should be: eels in *all i pebre,* that is to say, eels in a sauce made from garlic and pepper; made pungent — for the foreigners it is usually a little less so — which requires to be eaten with a good strong wine.

And if we go on to desserts, the reader can choose: fruit according to the season, always freshly picked; pastries and deep-fried buns, among them the *buñuelo,* especially sought after and consumed during the *fiestas* of Saint Joseph, and regarding refreshments, the *horchata de chufas* honours the fame which has been accorded it.

Valencian oranges also enjoy well-won universal praise. Beautiful on the outside and delicious inside.

THE SPECTACLES

The Valencian does not only enjoy himself on those days marked in red on the calendar. The city also offers places for entertainment: cinemas, theatres, dance halls, discotheques… and, as in the rest of Spanish cities… bullfights, performed in large, round arenas, and the Spanish national sport, football. The Valencians have always felt a great attraction towards the *Fiesta Nacional,* and among the native figures most sentimentally remembered by the town are the bullfight heroes Fabrilo and Granero, who were tragically killed in the ring. The bull-ring of Valencia, a short distance from the Caudillo ring and therefore in the centre of the city, is one of the biggest in Spain—its capacity is over 16,000 spectators—and undoubtedly, the most beautiful. It was built between 1850 and 1860 according to classical lines by the Roman amphitheatre at Nîmes. Two important fairs take place here —those of July and the Fallas—and many more bullfights during the season. Sometimes its arena serves for other popular spectacles, from comic bullfights to opera shows, so that the visitor and towns' people can always be sure of finding something to interest them.

There are two huge stadiums that belong to the two "historic" teams of the city. Extremely popular, it is very rare that matches do not reflect full attendance.

The bullfight ring of Valencia, in the centre of the city, has austere and sober lines. With its 384 arches on the outer part, and with its galleries, it is apparent that it has been modelled on the amphitheatre of Nîmes.

THE SOUTHERN PLAN

The city of Valencia has, over the years, suffered numerous devastating floods caused by the torrential currents of the river Turia, which destroyed everything found in its path. Those of 1957 reached such catastrophic proportions that a solution had to be studied by the government and Valencian technical teams capable of effectively resolving this problem. The decision required deep and thorough investigation, a laborious process whose result was the Law of the Southern Plan, 21st of December 1961.

It consisted of the diversion of the river bed, which at the same time would eliminate future risks of flooding and solve all the urban problems-access to the city, drainage, green zones... etc. All the problems which the rapidly expanding town had created. Today, with the extensive works now almost completely finished, the city of Valencia, sure of its successful future, is aware of how to lay the necessarily solid and well–considered foundations for the city of tomorrow.

The Southern Plan, a project that afforded Valencia with completely new horizons for urban development and which today is a splendid reality.

The purest artisan tradition and new technological advances blend together in the progressive industrial climate of Valencia. Fans, furniture, ceramic objects, dolls, oranges... Valencia's fame extends far beyond the frontiers of Spain and the city enjoys a well-deserved recognition on an international scale.

Picture of the Virgin del Puig, declared by King James I to be patroness of the Kingdom of Valencia. It is a beautiful high relief of Florentine style of the earlier part of the 14th century, considered to be a work of Juan Pisano, although tradition holds it to be miraculously similar to San Pedro Nolasco in 1237, a little before the reconquest of Valencia.

BENVINGUT SIGA QUI A SA CASA VE

"Welcome is anyone who comes to this house". With this popular expression of hospitality, which we ought to have said at the beginning, we now say farewell to our visitor, expressing, not only our wish that he has felt at home, but also our pleasure of having had him as a guest, and also express our sincere desire that he arrives safely to his own lands. The visit to Valencia has arrived at an end. We could still see many things but there will be time, no doubt, to repeat these walks and then we shall pause in front of buildings and in corners as yet hardly glanced at. On returning to his land, the visitor will be able to complete the sights which arise from the city, depending on which route he takes. Towards the south he will find Cullera, with rocky and sandy beaches; Gandia, with a beach that encourages bathing, and set in the middle of a beautiful orchard. If he went inland he would cross the Valencian Castilla, travelling through the famous wine producing vineyards. But if he goes to the north, he must stop before getting to Sagunto, with its ruins of a Roman theatre, here, in El Puig; between the 13th and 16th centuries, a Mercedarian monastery was built where the army of King James I camped before starting the campaign to recapture Valencia from the Moslems.

The Monastery of El Puig commemorates the conquest of Valencia by King James I. The Valencians see this spot as the heart of the Old Kingdom. The Gothic Church, of the 14th century, was well restored a short time ago.

Contents

That ancient part of history which is Spain is often referred to as "the bull's skin", because that is the shape of Spain on the map. The aim of this book is to present a detailed and comprehensive picture of a fragment of that "bull's skin", and to help this it includes a number of spectacular photographs. The Editor will be well satisfied if he has succeeded in giving you a deeper and better knowledge of Spain.

The printing of this book was completed
in the workshops of FISA - Industrias
Gráficas, Palaudarias, 26 - Barcelona
(Spain)